Who Is
Harry Potter?

Frans Lutters

Who Is Harry Potter?

Translated by Philip Mees

Published by:

Waldorf Publications at the
Research Institute for Waldorf Education
38 Main Street
Chatham, New York 12037

Title: *Who Is Harry Potter?*
Author: Frans Lutters
Translation: Philip Mees
Layout/design: Ann Erwin
Proofreading: Colleen Shetland
Cover design adapted from the original Dutch cover
    by Michiel Wijnbergh
ISBN #978-1-936367-69-6
© 2015 Waldorf Publications

Originally published in Dutch as *Wie is Harry Potter?*
© 2011 Frans Lutters / Uitgeverij Pentagon, Amsterdam
www.uitverijpentagon
info@uitgeverijpentagon.nlby
ISBN # 978-94-90455-23-1

Table of Contents

This booklet is dedicated to my students at the
Waldorf School in Zeist, Holland
whose interest in Harry Potter led me to
keep wondering about his identity
and the reality behind the story.

– Frans Lutters
Driebergen, Netherlands
May 2011

Introduction

In 1997 the first of the seven-volume series of Harry Potter books was published in England. And in July 2011 the film version of the last volume, *Harry Potter and the Deathly Hallows*, came out in movie theaters. This marked the end of a period of fourteen successive years in which books and movies about Harry Potter were published. All over the world many children, young and old, have followed the adventures of Harry Potter. They awaited the publication of the new installments and, together with their parents, stood in front of the bookstores the night before, full of expectation. And when the movies came out, millions of children and adults immersed themselves again in these same adventures.

The books have been published and read in more than 65 languages throughout the world. Never has a book circulated so fast. In the United States and Great Britain alone, 11 million copies of *Harry Potter and the Deathly Hallows* found their way to expectant readers in only one day. Every new installment broke the sales record of the previous one. Day and night people were reading, and non-English speaking children who could not wait for a translation taught themselves English through reading these books. Because of these unrivaled records, if for no other reason, Harry Potter became a phenomenon without equal in the history of humanity.

The British author Joanne K. Rowling was born on July 31, 1965, in the vicinity of Bristol, England. She wrote the first volume of the Harry Potter series in a café in Edinburgh, Scotland. She was a single mom living on welfare. One day after she had been writing, she left the café and heard a voice that made a deep impression: "The difficult thing will be to get it published. But if it is published it will be huge."[1] True enough, when she finished the manuscript, there was no publisher willing to print it. Twelve publishers refused, but Joanne kept trying. In 1997 *Harry Potter and the Philosopher's Stone* came out at Bloomsbury Publishing in England. Three days later the American publisher Scholastic offered Rowling $100,000 for the American publication rights.

A year later I saw the Dutch translation of *Harry Potter and the Philosopher's Stone*[2] in a bookshop. The title appealed to me; I pulled it off the shelf and took a look at it. My first impression was disappointing. That bourgeois, English atmosphere—did that have anything to do with alchemy and spirituality? I put the book back, not knowing that a few weeks later it would cross my path again. When I came back to school after a bout with the flu, the book was lying on my desk. The children, whose class teacher I was at the time, had suddenly gone crazy about Harry Potter. Despite my doubts, the children succeeded in convincing me that it was important to read this book to them. That was the beginning of my journey into an uninterrupted, magical adventure with Harry Potter, the deeper truth of which began to reveal itself to me over the course of the past few years.

I began to wonder whether the inspiration Joanne Rowling received should be viewed as just fiction. Or was her intuitive encounter with Harry Potter in 1990, during a train trip from Manchester to London, a revelation of a reality that is actually taking place in our time?[3] What was

8

the reality behind the face of the boy Joanne Rowling saw in the rain-spattered window of her train compartment? And how is it possible that, during this now-famous trip, she could experience the life and complex adventures of Harry Potter and his friends so completely that the result has been seven big books, a total of almost 4400 pages? She says herself that perhaps her encounter with Harry Potter during the train trip was not fiction but reality: "The idea of the Harry Potter books arose in a train."[4] She goes on to say that she did not aim for sorcery and magic, but that sorcery and magic sought her out. The question about Harry's world is: "What if it were true?"

As I read I was more and more surprised and had more and more questions. I soon realized that what was touching me so deeply was the personality of Harry Potter, by himself and together with his close friends Ron and Hermione. Harry Potter is the kind of boy we all know: unspectacular but with a good heart, honest and spontaneous. He likes adventures and sometimes does thoughtless things. But what makes him exceptional is that he is called to great deeds. His life takes a dramatic turn on the eve of his eleventh birthday when he is visited by a gigantic man called Rubeus Hagrid, the first magician Harry consciously meets. Hagrid hands Harry a letter inviting him to continue his education at the Hogwarts School of Witchcraft and Wizardry. Harry accepts and travels to Hogwarts. Thus it is Hagrid, a hairy, wild-looking half-giant, who becomes Harry's guardian and conducts him safely across the threshold between the world of Muggles, the people who lack magical capacities, and the magical world of Hogwarts. Active in the borderland between both worlds, Rubeus Hagrid is the perfect guardian and watchman for Harry Potter.

In the course of the years at Hogwarts, Harry goes through an intensive schooling during which he develops his magical capacities. This takes him more and more to the center of a great conflict between good and dark powers. Clearly, in a world unknown to ordinary people but which borders on everyday reality, an enormous battle is taking place between good and evil, between white and black magicians. Harry proves to be the center point of this battle, as witnessed by the puzzling scar on his forehead. It is impressive to experience how Harry, with Ron and Hermione at his side, and in spite of all the attacks and temptations, always keeps striving for the good. Even in the greatest doubt and in the most trying circumstances, he remains true to himself. The evil powers fight him with all their strength through black magic, but Harry marvelously holds his ground. He carries a strength in himself that envelops and protects him.

I kept asking myself: Who is Harry Potter? Is he perhaps more than a hero arising from Joanne Rowling's imagination? What made the young writer's encounter with Harry during that long, rainy train trip so real and unforgettably intense? Questions like these led me in the course of years to my discovering the real Harry Potter. The events described in the books do not take place outside of time; they are set by Joanne Rowling in the years 1991 to 1998. At the beginning of the series this is not obvious, but it is clarified in a passage in the last volume, and I will elucidate on this timeframe later in this booklet. I am convinced that Harry is going about somewhere in the world at this very moment, and that he is now [2011] thirty-one years old. Consequently, more questions arise: "How is he doing today? What is he up to now? What about his future?" To these questions I have also found answers that have become more and more clear. It appears that the story of Harry Potter has not yet come to an end.

I believe my discoveries are significant for everyone who, reading the books and watching the movies, has befriended Harry Potter. But if you don't yet know him, or have an aversion to the books and movies, this little book is perhaps still worth reading. I assert that the real Harry Potter, together with his friends, is currently engaged in an actual battle which is very much our business, which is veiled by popular opinion and the media, and which demands to be brought into the light of day. Hence this booklet: a call to take Harry seriously. Harry is our contemporary.

In her descriptions of his adventures, Joanne Rowling has supplied us with a great deal of information about him and his world, even if often between the lines. This information has been systematically ordered and presented in numerous books and websites of which I have made grateful use.

1

The Battle for Hogwarts

The Hogwarts coat of arms:
"Never Tickle a Sleeping Dragon"

Harry travels on the Hogwarts Express from King's Cross Station in London to Hogwarts, the School of Witchcraft and Wizardry. The train departs with all the students every year on the same date, September 1, from platform 9¾. Platform 9¾ is hard to find because it is not visible to materialistically-inclined people, i.e., Muggles. It is situated between platforms 9 and 10, between normally visible things, and you need a bit of magician's blood in your veins to discover it. This means that you can find the way to Hogwarts only with clairvoyant capacities.

Since the year 1899, every human being has had the capacity to develop clairvoyance. In occult tradition, 1899 brought the end of Kali Yuga, the dark age, during which only a few people, such as alchemists and Rosicrucians, were able to develop clairvoyance. The year 1899 was the transition to a new era, the era of light, in which it became possible to develop a new form of clairvoyance out of our own forces. Albus Dumbledore, the great magician and headmaster of Hogwarts, began his studies on September 1, 1892, when he, like Harry and the other pupils, had just turned 11 years of age, and he completed his training at Hogwarts in 1899.

This new clairvoyance is connected in our time with our learning to perceive a delicate etheric world which has always permeated the outer world, but gradually became invisible for Muggles, materialistic people. Alchemists have always known that the outer world is permeated by forces that are invisible to our normal senses, and they distinguished four groups connected to the four elements: fire, air, water and earth. The delicate warmth ether permeates fire; light ether is present in air; chemical ether is in everything fluid; and life ether gives form to solid matter. In clairvoyance there is always a tendency to give preference to one of these four. This preference shows up already in childhood, but precisely in the eleventh year, the temperament becomes the medium through which the child learns to learn and work out of the four elements. Fire lives in choleric children, earth in the melancholic ones, the airy in the sanguine and the fluid, watery element in the phlegmatic ones.

The four Houses to which the new pupils are assigned upon arrival by the Sorting Hat are related to these four aspects of the etheric world. The Sorting Hat, which the new pupils of Hogwarts have to put on their heads, analyzes the free ether around each head and then assigns each to the group to which he or she shows the closest relationship. These four groups all have their own quadrant in the coat of arms of Hogwarts. Harry is assigned to Griffindor, which has the courageous lion as its emblem. The serpent is the sign of the crafty, materialistically-oriented Slytherin group; the badger that of the industrious, watery Hufflepuff; and the eagle with its light intelligence belongs to Ravenclaw.

Since the founding of Hogwarts more than a thousand years ago, good and evil have converged and mingled there. Located at the edge of the inhabited world, the school has connections to both the material and the spiritual worlds. It is a characteristic of Anglo-Saxon occultism that spiritual reality takes on materialistic forms; there is always a tendency toward a kind of spiritual materialism. This presents a great danger because it opens the door to black magic, which aims to seize power over humanity. This form of black magic is brought into the School of Witchcraft and Wizardry by Voldemort, the greatest black magician of all time, and his henchmen. While Voldemort infiltrates the school with his servants and threatens Harry's life, the white magician Dumbledore is the headmaster of the school and the great advisor to Harry.

For Albus Dumbledore, Joanne Rowling used as her model Alfred Dunn, the principal of her own school, the St. Michael School in Winterbourne. This grade school dates back to 1813 and was originally located above the pub *George and Dragon*. Can you imagine anything more picturesque? In the Middle Ages, the battle of St. George with the dragon was seen as an earthly reflection of the battle between the archangel Michael and the powers of evil in the spiritual world. Since time immemorial, Michael has been related with the powers of the sun. In the Middle Ages, intelligence was always experienced as connected with the light, life and warmth of the sun. The old professors at the universities of Paris and Cologne still knew that Michael brings cosmic intelligence into the soul of the human being. The old professors knew that Michael, as the guardian of cosmic intelligence, accompanied the development of philosophy. But they also knew that the new age of discoveries and inventions, beginning in the 15th century, inaugurated a new era in which Michael, out of respect for human freedom, would leave the control of intelligence to the responsibility of the individual human being.

However, a problem arose: The dark powers, often depicted as a dragon, tried to seize the now-freed intelligence. The 15th century legend of Faust, the professor and mage, shows how an intellectually developed human being enters into a covenant with the power of evil. Five centuries later this dark power steps into the story of Harry Potter with even greater forces as Lord Voldemort. That means that this happens in our time, for Harry Potter is our contemporary. At Hogwarts good and evil do battle with each other in their representatives of Albus Dumbledore and Voldemort. They fight with the forces of light and those of darkness for control of the intelligence that has been freed by Michael and entrusted by him to the human being. This is not just a battle for the future of Hogwarts; the future of humanity is at stake, and the battle is fierce.

Hermione, Harry's classmate and inseparable com-panion, is a marvelous example of someone who, with her impressive intelligence, wants to serve the good through thick and thin. Draco Malfoy, on the other hand, is a boy who uses his intelligence in a dark way, mostly for his own purposes. From the very first day, he challenges and threatens Harry with spiteful tricks and mean jokes. While Hermione is connected with Albus Dumbledore, Draco comes more and more under the influence of Voldemort. Dumbledore is the school's unyielding representative of the archangel Michael, while Voldemort reveals himself in the course of the book series as an incarnation of Ahriman, the Persian name Rudolf Steiner adopted for the power of darkness.

> Thus behind the scenes of existence is raging the
> battle of Michael against all that is of Ahriman.[5]

Just like Michael, Dumbledore does not want to gather intelligence for himself, but strives to bring it to development in such a way that it benefits everyone. He uses his power with great circumspection and reluctance, and he respects the freedom of his students. What Rudolf Steiner said about the battle between Michael and Ahriman fully applies to the struggle between Dumbledore and Voldemort:

> Truth to tell, Ahriman has a most contemptuous
> judgment of Michael. He thinks Michael foolish
> and stupid—stupid, needless to say, in relation to
> himself. For Michael does not wish to seize the
> Intelligence and make it personally his own. Michael
> only wills, and has willed through the thousands
> of years, nay through the aeons, to administer the
> Pan-Intelligence. And now once more, now that
> human beings have the Intelligence, it should again
> be administered by Michael as something belonging
> to all mankind—as the common and universal
> Intelligence that benefits all human beings alike.[6]

2

The Story Takes Place in Our Time

Since the death of his parents in his earliest childhood, Harry Potter has lived with his maternal Aunt Petunia's family, the Dursleys. In the first chapter of each book, Joanne Rowling sketches how this family is totally lacking in spirit. This is a family where everything has to be plain and average, a small world where the only things that count are composure and material well-being. Thus, in the beginning of the first book, *Harry Potter and the Philosopher's Stone*, we are shown a family where there is no space for the human spirit. "Spirits are scary and vague!" The realm of spirit is so threatening to Mr. and Mrs. Dursley that it is better not to get involved with it. Adventures and questions about life are forcefully avoided. For Harry this is a real trial. There is no room for spiritual matters, and whenever Harry has a question of this kind, he is told, with vicious mockery, to shut up.

In this situation Harry unknowingly encounters the consequences of a forgotten but important ecclesiastical Council that took place more than a thousand years ago in Constantinople (now Istanbul, Turkey) in the years 869–870. The decisions made there by bishops and cardinals continue to affect the daily reality of Harry Potter and his foster family. What happened at this Council?

On February 27, 870, after ten sessions, the decision was made in the Hagia Sophia Cathedral that Christians would no longer be allowed to speak of "the spirit of the human being." Rudolf Steiner (1861–1925), founder of anthroposophy, was a proponent of a threefold image of the human being in which body, soul and spirit were recognized. He described the event of the Council of Constantinople as follows:

> [...] the Catholic Church, which was strongly influenced by the remnants of the impulses from the Academy of Gondishapur, decreed dogmatically at the eighth Ecumenical Council in Constantinople that it is not necessary to believe in the spirit. [...] The new dogma that was instituted at that time stipulates that believing in the spirit is not necessary; believing in body and soul is fully sufficient. In addition, it was stipulated that the soul has something spirit-like in it also.[7]

The spirit was literally abolished! In our time this view and attitude toward life have become decisive for all scientific thinking about man and world.

Now, it is a remarkable fact that, in all seven Harry Potter books, Joanne Rowling places the story of Harry's battle against Voldemort squarely in our time. The seven books, published between 1997 and 2007, place Harry's seven school years at Hogwarts from 1991 to 1998. That becomes clear in the last book, *Harry Potter and the Deathly Hallows*, when Harry arrives at the place where his parents were killed by Voldemort and sees a sign with the following text:

> On this spot, on the night of 31 October 1981,
> Lily and James Potter lost their lives.

Their son, Harry, remains the only wizard
ever to have survived the Killing Curse.
This house, invisible to Muggles, has been left
in its ruined state as a monument to the Potters
and as a reminder of the violence
that tore apart their family.

Harry knows that he had already been the object of a fight with Voldemort when he was but a year old, in the First Wizarding War of 1970–1981. Taking into account that Harry was eleven when Hagrid invited him to Hogwarts by order of Dumbledore, the first book is therefore set in the year 1991. Thus we arrive at the following chronology of the books:

Harry Potter and the Philosopher's Stone 1991–1992
Harry Potter and the Chamber of Secrets 1992–1993
Harry Potter and the Prisoner of Azkaban 1993–1994
Harry Potter and the Goblet of Fire 1994–1995
Harry Potter and the Order of the Phoenix 1995–1996
Harry Potter and the Half-Blood Prince 1996–1997
Harry Potter and the Deathly Hallows 1997–1998

Because of his upbringing in the spiritless Dursley family, Harry Potter shares the destiny of countless children of our time who cannot find a way to connect the spiritual intentions with which they are born to the world in which they live. But in his destiny he has the strength to break through the boundary between the material and spiritual worlds; in some way he is awake and asks himself many questions. And that is something his foster parents and cousin do not appreciate in him!

The turning point in his life—his coming to Hogwarts— makes Harry deeply happy. He learns to see his goal: to participate in the battle between light and darkness. He enters a world that was hidden from humanity for generations, and he is given a goal in his school years of enriching his intelligence with new spiritual capacities in a powerful way. He also experiences, however, that light and darkness are often commingled. There are certain teachers in the school who are influenced by black magic. Because Voldemort's power is growing in the school and in the world, the battle between light and darkness in the Harry Potter books becomes increasingly fierce. It is Dumbledore who is able to push back the black magic in Hogwarts.

Long before Harry was born, Dumbledore was already actively working to maintain inner and outer freedom. The events that preceded Harry's adventures in fact take up a good part of the 20th century: Voldemort tried to establish a dictatorship of the dark magicians over the world. In this he got help from demons of darkness, the spirit-killing Death Eaters. In the First Wizarding War, the ones who took their stand against Voldemort and his followers were primarily the members of the Order of the Phoenix, headed by Dumbledore; Harry's parents belonged to the Order. Voldemort attacked and killed Harry's parents, but ironically, the Killing Curse he hurled at little Harry ricocheted back to him and he lost not only the battle but his material being.

Voldemort did not die, but from that moment lived as a specter in a condition between life and death. This is explained more fully in the last book of the series, *Harry Potter and the Deathly Hallows*: Voldemort splits off parts of his soul and hides these through black magical practices in amulets and objects called Horcruxes. Harry, too, carries part of Voldemort in his head, right behind the scar on his forehead, where he was hit by Voldemort's curse when he was a baby. The scar has the shape of a lightning bolt and causes a searing, unbearable pain whenever Voldemort is nearby. Voldemort does not rest until he has found a new body to incarnate in. Harry is confronted with these attempts in the first books of the series.

Prior to the First Wizarding War, Dumbledore had a confrontation with another dark magician, Gellert Grindelwald. Grindelwald possessed an extremely powerful magic wand, the Elder Wand, which ended up making everyone who possessed it hunger for power, and then it destroyed them. His intention was to establish a magical dictatorship over all Muggles. But he was defeated by Dumbledore in a legendary duel in 1945 and forced to relinquish this wand to Dumbledore, who has the capacity to control its power.

According to Joanne Rowling, the battle in which Dumbledore defeats Grindelwald is a clear reference to the rise of National Socialism in Germany. In the *Book of Revelation*, St. John describes how a Beast rises up from the abyss, a Beast of great power who speaks blasphemy and is worshipped by the tribes and peoples of humanity (Chapter 13: 1–9). Rudolf Steiner points to this Beast in 1924 and connects it with the year 1933:

> Before the etheric Christ can be comprehended by human beings in the right way, humanity must first cope with encountering the Beast who will rise up in 1933.[8]

On January 30, 1933, Adolf Hitler became Chancellor of Germany; this marked the beginning of the Third Reich (Third Kingdom) and the persecution of the Jews. The working of the Beast rising up out of the abyss can be recognized in the deeds of Hitler and Himmler, the founder in 1930 and leader of the notorious magical order of the Schutzstaffel (SS).

For a long time Harry knows nothing of these conflicts. However, they prove to be of decisive importance in the battle he has to wage decades later. Dumbledore will not live to see the outcome of that fight. He dies during the battle in June 1997, and after Dumbledore's death, Voldemort goes after the Elder Wand. For Harry, the fact that he, as a modern Parzival, has to find his way without really knowing what he is doing, becomes a real trial. But he, just like Parzival, will get help in unexpected ways.

3
Who Is Harry Potter?

At the beginning of this book, I asked whether Joanne Rowling didn't have much deeper intentions with her spiritual-realistic epic than a more or less symbolic story about the eternal battle between good and evil. Out of this question I found a person in history who had the kind of access to the spiritual world that Harry has, and who also knew and experienced that the human being is involved in a battle between good and evil powers. I recognized Harry Potter in the life and legendary writings of Mani, who lived from 216 to 276 in the Middle East, and who perished in a conflict with dark magicians in Gondishapur in 276.

Mani was a great teacher of mildness and peace. Although the being of the Christ, as Sun Spirit, was central for him, he tried to bring the religions of his time together in one common vision. An extensive traveler, he knew and respected Buddhism, Hinduism and the teachings of Confucius and Zoroaster, and his doctrine has become the most widely-spread worldview in the area between Iraq and China.

Mani died in Gondishapur due to treason. Gondishapur had a famous academy where many philosophical, scientific and magical books were collected, studied and translated. The alchemical and natural scientific works of Aristotle, thought by most scholars to be lost, were known there, although interpreted in a one-sidedly intellectual manner. The spiritual intelligence of the human being was not recognized as an individual spiritual capacity. Thus one can say that Mani died in a city where, after his death, the "abolition of the spirit" was prepared through the development of scientific and magical insights.

Early in his work in anthroposophy, Rudolf Steiner gave an extensive description of the life and work of Mani:

> ... [T]he legend of Manichaeism is a great cosmic
> legend, a supersensible legend. It tells us that at
> one time the spirits of darkness wanted to take the
> kingdom of light by storm. They actually reached
> the borders of the kingdom of light and hoped to
> conquer it. But they failed to achieve anything.
> Now they were to be punished—and that is a very
> significant feature which I beg you to take account
> of—they were to be punished by the kingdom of
> light. But in this realm there was nothing that was in
> any way evil; there was only good. Thus the demons
> of darkness could be punished only with something
> good. So what happened? The spirits of light took
> a part of their own kingdom and mixed it with the
> materialized kingdom of darkness. Because there
> was now a part of the kingdom of light mingled
> with the kingdom of darkness, a leaven had been
> introduced into the kingdom of darkness, a ferment
> which produced a chaotic whirling dance, whereby
> it received a new element into itself, i.e., death.
> Therefore, it continually consumes itself and thus
> carries within itself the germ of its own destruction.
> It is further related that, because of this, the race
> of mankind was brought into existence: Primeval

man represents just what was sent down from the kingdom of light to mix with the kingdom of darkness and to conquer, through death, what should not have been there; to conquer it within his own being. The profound thought which lies in this is that the kingdom of darkness has to be overcome by the kingdom of light, not by means of punishment, but through mildness.[9]

By reading and rereading these words, I found confirmation of the correspondences between the life and struggles of Harry Potter and the vision and life task of Mani. As an infant already Harry inflamed the rage of Voldemort. His parents were killed by the Killing Curse. Harry is the only one who ever survived this curse. Even Dumbledore will die, and Harry is threatened with death all the time. But he is victorious! He achieves this not through power but through mildness. This is perhaps the most conspicuous characteristic Harry has in common with Mani, his predecessor of eighteen centuries. The recognition of the correspondences between the mission of Mani and that of Harry Potter led me to the answer to the question that is the title of this booklet: Who is Harry Potter?

According to Mani the conflict with the powers of darkness arose at the beginning of world evolution. Mani relates how the original human being was pure and pristine, but then is contaminated with evil. The primal human being, the originally good and pure human being, descends into the realm of darkness. Again and again Harry Potter is described as a boy who remains true to himself, and it is this characteristic that causes evil to "boil in a chaotic, whirling dance." He radiates goodness and mildness even in the deepest darkness of evil. This throws Voldemort and his followers into a flaming rage.

The Dutch scientist of religion, Hans Jonas, describes how it is possible that, in the vision of Mani, light and darkness are engaged in such a roundabout war with each other:

> The place of light borders immediately on that of darkness, without any separation. That is ground zero of the doctrine. All descriptions of Mani's doctrine begin with this contraposition of the two primeval powers. Persian Manicheans, who adhere to Zoroastrian traditions, call the personified darkness Ahriman.[10]

This inexorable, direct relationship also characterizes the battle Harry Potter and his friends have to wage.

Later I will go deeper into the relationship between Mani and Harry Potter, but here I already want to raise one important aspect. Until his death in June 1997, the leader of the battle against Voldemort is Albus Dumbledore. This good magician, born in 1881, is then 116 years old and thus has reached the outer limit of a human life. It was Dumbledore who brought Voldemort to Hogwarts, when the latter was living an unhappy existence in an orphanage as a child named Tom Riddle. Dumbledore was then Tom's teacher in Transfiguration, the art of changing shape. And trans-figuration is what Dumbledore had always hoped to achieve with Voldemort ever since his boyhood years—alas, in vain.

Here we come to a central Manichaean motif: *not the subjection of evil, but its transformation.* In Manichaeism transformation of the human being can take place only with the help of the "spiritual being of the sun" which Mani worshipped as the Christ. The future of the pure life force of the human being is guarded from the hardening dark powers of Ahriman by this Sun Being.

In the final confrontation of Harry and Voldemort, in the seventh book, three very powerful objects play a central role. These are the Deathly Hallows, relics of death: the magic Elder Wand, the Cloak of Invisibility and the Resurrection Stone. Harry withstands the temptation to use these objects as instruments of power and is able to release them from their black magical working by using them for the good. Thus the "relics of death" become "relics of life."

The Elder Wand, Resurrection Stone and Cloak of Invisibility, united in a black magical sign

Mani strove toward the transformation of evil through mildness. At the beginning of the 20th century, the deeper secrets of Mani's confrontation with the powers of darkness could be discussed by Rudolf Steiner only in part because people were not yet strong enough to deal with them fully.

With the publication of the Harry Potter books beginning in 1997, the time has come when it is necessary that young people become acquainted at an early age with this transformation of evil. Children worldwide have shown this themselves by buying and reading—and rereading— the books in unprecedented numbers.

4

An Informative Visit

In the spring of 2005 everyone was in great expectation
of *Harry Potter and the Half-Blood Prince*. There were rumors
that someone, perhaps even Dumbledore, was going to die
in this book. I was visiting Professor Gilles Quispel,[11] who
fought all his life for truth and openness in spiritual research.*
He was a champion of a spiritual Christianity that had been
hidden for centuries under the sands of the Egyptian desert.
In the 1950s he had in his room a copy of the *Codex Jung*, a
magical book that had long been hidden. Now, fifty years later,
the *Codex Jung* has been published together with all the other
codices from the Nag Hammadi finds of 1945. This came
about thanks to the joint commitment of three individuals:
Carl Gustav Jung, Queen Juliana of The Netherlands and,
last but not least, Gilles Quispel. This was the subject about
which I wanted to see him.

"Nice of you to come. There has been interest in Mani
for a long time. During World War II already some good
anthroposophical books appeared on Mani. Of course, I don't
take credit for Rudolf Steiner's vision of him," he said with
an appreciative smile. "Manichaeism is a church, a Christian
church or, which is perhaps interesting for your readers, a

---

*He died unexpectedly in 2006 in Egypt, the country which had
been so important for him.

29

Christian community. With one single exception, it existed without schisms for a thousand years. No splits, no heresies. And yet, this church encompassed an area that stretched from the Atlantic to the Pacific Ocean. This was because Mani himself had put his entire teaching in writing. Everything was anchored in his written works. Manichaeism is the simplest religion in extremely complex clothing. It has its foundation in the thought: The spirit saves the soul out of matter!* The soul is kindred to God. In the soul lives the spiritual-divine in the human being. This is a great difference in conception as compared with the other principal Christian streams. In the Manichaen view, the human being is a spiritual being. Through his self-realization he helps God. The human being helps God realize His plan. According to the Manichaeans, God is Being in Movement. This is also the view of the German philosopher Hegel, the German idealists, and also that of Rudolf Steiner!"

Gilles Quispel went on to say that he spoke often at the Goetheanum, the anthroposophical center in Dornach, Switzerland. During youth conferences he related easily to the young people, for he had a lot of experience with students. Laughing, he described how, when the applause after one of his lectures did not want to stop, he threw the flowers of the bouquet he had received into the hall. I asked whether it would be important to tell young people about Mani. "It depends," was his answer. "It would be, if you told your students about a Christian church that practiced non-violence, that never took up the sword and that was the most persecuted religion in the world—persecuted by Islam, the other Christian churches and even by Buddhism. Christianity, as it lived in Mani, was based

---

*This is in contrast to Protestant and Catholic thought.

on the Sermon on the Mount. The content of the Sermon on the Mount is the only sensible way to deal with violence." I recognized the character of Harry Potter immediately from this description of Mani and his followers.

"In a similar way the Russian painter Marc Chagall showed himself a real Gnostic when he was asked to design new windows for the church in Mainz, which had been bombed by the Allied air force. At first, this was a problem for him, a Jew, but his wife advised him to wait with his answer to see if he would be asked again. When that happened he agreed, and he made windows for a church in a city in Germany, the country that had done so much harm to his people. Gnosis is sometimes accused of not being ethical. Marc Chagall proves the contrary."

Later Gilles Quispel showed me his shrine. Besides pictures of his loved ones, there was a reproduction of a painting by Chagall of the three angels that visited Abraham, shining white against a deep red background. There was also a picture of Solzhenitsyn, whom he called the greatest martyr of our time. With his 89 years, Gilles Quispel let me know he was getting tired and that it was time for his rest and a cup of tea. Suddenly it was as if I were sitting in the room with Dumbledore. Would he know where the real Harry Potter is?

"The *Codex Jung* stood here in this room. And then we had the finds in Qumran, the Gnostics, Nag Hammadi and the Mani Codex. It is my view that it is God's will that they become known in our time. You could see it as a process of synchronicity, or as destiny—I don't care—I see it as God's hand. Jung also fully realized this. Jung's psychology gives us the possibility to understand these writings, for instance, the concept of androgyny that is at the basis of the Gospel of Thomas. Tertullian made fun of it, and Valentine talked about the human being who had to become a bride. But Jung provided the key with his concepts of *Animus* and *Anima*.

"There are always people who want to quarrel and fight, also around the *Codex Jung*. I bought this codex in Egypt in 1952 when I was 36 and was already a professor. In 1953 I negotiated in Egypt for the other codices from the Nag Hammadi find; they were kept in the Coptic Museum in Cairo and were not released for study or publication. I was promised that all the codices would be published in exchange for the *Codex Jung*. I was the first to receive a copy of the Gospel of Thomas, which I then published."

Together with his wife, Gilles Quispel traveled to many countries and told the story about the streams which, when compared to mainstream Christianity, seemed to be the losers. Many people were interested. I realized that, due in part to the work of this remarkable human being, the losers of the past could be found again. Yes, Dumbledore may have died in the battle, but the effects of his work continue. This kind and very awake scholar attested to that.[12]

5

The Life of Mani

In time, I have gradually become more and more confirmed in my conviction that in Harry Potter the impulse of Mani is becoming active again in our time. The Cologne Mani Codex became accessible to the general public in 2005, through of the efforts of the Dutch professor Gilles Quispel.[13] This Mani Codex, which is a tiny little book less than two inches long, gives us much information on the life of Mani.

Mani, the prophet.
Interpretation by a present-day artist

Mani was born in 216 in the vicinity of Baghdad. His parents probably belonged to the nobility and were followers of the Jewish prophet Elchasai, whose name may mean "hidden strength." This group was strongly connected with the impulse of baptism in the tradition of John the Baptist.

As a child Mani was already clairvoyant. In many studies about him there is mention of his receiving revelations. He had contact with the reality of the spiritual world.

In his twelfth year, at that time the year of religious adulthood, Mani had a remarkable spiritual experience that was mediated by his *Syzygos*, his "twin companion." In his own book, *Shabuhragan*, he described his experiences of that year of his life:

> Then the Living Paraclete descended to me and
> addressed me. He revealed to me the secret mystery
> that was hidden for the worlds and the generations:
> the mystery of the Depth and the Height; he
> revealed to me the mystery of Light and Darkness,
> the mystery of the battle and the great war caused
> by the Darkness. He revealed to me how, when they
> mingled, the Light pushed the Darkness back.[14]

Through his encounter with the *Syzygos*, wrote Mani, "I saw the All and I became a body and a spirit." He knew then that he had been called for a special mission.

When he was 24, and after this event was repeated, Mani took leave of the community of Elchasaites with their purification rituals. He went to India and, upon his return, entered into the service of King Shapur I. This Persian ruler founded the city of Gondishapur in 271. At Shapur's court, Mani became his most important spiritual counselor. However, he also ran into strong opposition from dark mages at court, followers of the by now rigidified and dogmatic doctrine of Zarathustra. But Mani knew Zarathustra as a predecessor and fellow warrior, and he strove to integrate

Zarathustra's teaching with that of Buddha into a tolerant and magical Christianity:

> From eon to eon, the apostles of God have not
> ceased to proclaim the wisdom and works. Thus
> they came in one era in the lands of India through
> the apostle that was Buddha, and in another era in
> the land of Iran through Zarathustra.[15]

In this period, the teaching of Mani started to spread all over Asia. A strong social community developed in which twelve bishops and seventy-two deacons acted as spiritual leaders. But the relationship with King Shapur I was broken when his son became ill and Mani was asked to cure him, for Mani was unable to prevent the death of the son. As a result he was thrown into prison. Albert Steffen described in his drama *The Death Experience of Manes* how Mani during the night had an experience of himself as "the Youth of Nain" who was resurrected from death by Christ (Luke 7: 11–17).

When one of the guards let him escape, Mani again traveled far and wide. He returned to court in 273 after King Shapur was succeeded by his son Hormazd I, but after the latter's sudden death in 276, he was once more convicted and put into prison. Heavy chains were put on his neck, legs and wrists. Slowly he weakened. Then he was flayed alive and his skin was stuffed with herbs and hung on the city wall of Gondishapur as a "warning to braggarts." Several centuries after this martyrdom, in the year 666, Gondishapur reached its dark zenith.

6

Harry and Mani

Just like Harry, Mani stood in the middle of the battle with the powers of darkness. There are striking parallels between the traditions regarding Mani and the pictures Joanne Rowling gives us in the story of Harry Potter. For both of them the battle began in their twelfth year. We have already seen that at that age Mani had a remarkable spiritual experience mediated by his *Syzygos*, his heavenly twin companion:

> Just like that warrior ... I said, "You have ... and from your hand ... and other things you have given me [and] brought to me." And even now he himself accompanies me, and he himself keeps and protects me. And in his power I fight with Âz and Ahriman and teach men wisdom and knowledge and save them from Âz and Ahriman.[16]

Harry receives the first message from Hogwarts on the day he begins the twelfth year of his life. On that day he also receives from Hagrid, the watchman of Hogwarts, the white owl Hedwig, as a sign of his first contact with the reality of the spiritual world. Soon after, he enters the world which is closed and unknown to ordinary people, Muggles. He starts on a path as a "warrior," a path on which he battles "against Âz and Ahriman."

Both Mani and Harry are confronted with the fact that evil takes place in multiple layers. In Voldemort, for instance, and his connection with the Death Eaters, we can recognize the hardening tendency of Ahriman. But possibly Voldemort fights also out of a deeper layer of evil, the Asuras. This evil power wishes to shatter the "I" of the human being. This is exactly what Voldemort did with the black magical methods of the Horcruxes. He split off parts of his own soul.

We have seen how Mani indicates that in relation to the *Syzygos* he "saw the All and became a body and a spirit." Harry experiences something similar most clearly in his performance during the Quidditch games. Harry is agile and fast in this unusual magicians' sport, and especially fast in the unity of body and spirit. With enormous presence of mind, he follows the Snitch, a winged golden ball. This is, from time immemorial, the picture of the higher "I"; it also stands on the staff of Hermes, the Caduceus.

Eventually we will see that hidden inside the Snitch, which becomes Harry's property, is the *Resurrection Stone*. This enables beloved persons who have died to enter into earthly reality and support Harry in the great final battle against Voldemort. This secret is not revealed until the seventh book when Harry is eighteen years old and will soon finish his school years at Hogwarts. After that, he must stand completely on his own feet and build a lasting connection with the spiritual world without any further assistance. At that moment his beloved helper, the owl Hedwig, dies.

When the Snitch opens and Harry finds the Resurrection Stone, he encounters people who had always been his protectors in the background: his father James Potter, his mother

Lily, his godfather Sirius Black and his teacher Remus Lupin. After the Snitch of his own individuality, his higher "I," which has gone through many lives, has opened itself for his consciousness, Harry can meet them again in their destiny connection with him.

Cyril of Alexandria (378–444) relates a tradition about Mani that shows that he also stood in a continuous spiritual stream. This legend follows Skythianos and Terebinthus, in the latter of which the Buddha (563–483 BC), was working. Rudolf Steiner also quotes this tradition:

> Mani, or Manes, the founder of Manichaeism, appeared in the third century AD in Babylon. An unusual legend has the following to say about him: Skythianos and Terebinthus, or Buddha, were his predecessors. The latter was the pupil of the former. After the violent death of Skythianos, Terebinthus fled with the books to Babylon. He also suffered misfortune; the only one to accept his teaching was an elderly widow. She inherited his books and left them, at her death, to her foster-child, a twelve-year-old boy whom she had adopted out of slavery when he was seven years old.[17]

This transfer of books can be seen as a picture of a spiritual connection: Mani received an inheritance from two spiritual teachers, Skythianos and Terebinthus. Later we will go deeper into the role of these individuals in the spiritual development of humanity. We will also explore the persons around Harry who carry the signature of these spiritual leaders of humanity.

7

Three Times 666

The struggles in the seven Harry Potter books culminate in 1998. There is something significant about this number, although it may not be obvious at first sight. The year 1998 can be understood as three times 666. In the Middle Ages in Europe the number 666 was seen as the number of the being of evil. We read in the Book of Revelation (13:18):

> This calls for wisdom. If anyone has insight, let him calculate the number of the beast, for it is man's number. His number is 666.

Early Christians connected this number of the beast with Emperor Nero, who killed so many Christians. Later the number was connected with the year 666. And indeed, in 666 for the first time wisdom was required to recognize the beast. It was working with great intelligence out of the famous Academy of Gondishapur in Babylonia, a school led by mages in the tradition of Zarathustra, and in which all philosophy and magic from the ancient world were collected. At a certain time a dark magician became its leader. Rudolf Steiner said about him that, although his name remained unknown, he was the greatest opponent of Christ Jesus. This reminds us of the way Voldemort was referred to: "He who must not be named." That which this magician in Gondishapur intended to achieve through his teaching to his pupils, however, was not achieved.[18] And yet, the dark wisdom from the school of Gondishapur had great after-effects, such as the decision of the eighth Ecumenical Council (in Constantinople, 870) to abolish the spirit.

The year 1332, two times 666, also falls in a period of battles between light and dark powers. In this period the Order of the Templars ceased to exist, as a result of the manipulations of King Philip the Fair of France and Pope Clemens V. Philip the Fair worked out of the power of evil; he lusted for gold. During his reign the Templars were the bankers of Europe and possessed incredible amounts of gold, which they strove to put to use for the benefit of human society. As Rudolf Steiner indicated, they worked out of the impulse of Mani, as did the Cathars who were so viciously persecuted in the south of France:

> This Mani was the founder of a spiritual movement
> which, although at first only a small sect, became
> a mighty spiritual current. The Albigenses,
> Waldenses and Cathars of the Middle Ages are the
> continuation of this current, to which also belong
> the Knights Templar ...[19]

Philip knew how to torture the Templars during the trials in order to evoke delusional images in them and so force them into confessions. "A highly gifted personality, Philip the Fair, who was equipped with an extraordinary degree of cunning and the most evil ahrimanic wisdom, had access to this inspiration through gold."[20] Voldemort tries all the time to do the same thing with Harry and his other victims.

The secret of Voldemort has to do with the impulse that seems to raise its ugly head in the development of humanity every 666 years. The great renaissance scholar and magician Agrippa von Nettesheim (1486–1535) connected the number 666 with the anti-sun forces in the cosmos. He gave the name of the being that hides behind this impulse: Sorat.[21] Rudolf Steiner also used this name to describe the demonic sun being, the sun demon. He describes how Sorat works black-magically by mingling spiritual and material forces in such a way that they produce an enormously strong, suggestive effect.

Three times 666 brings us to the year 1998, Harry's last school year at Hogwarts, in which Voldemort's power reaches its culmination, although he is ultimately defeated. What determining and suggestive spiritual-material force do we have in our time that threatens to dominate humanity? We could think of the increasing digitalization of our lives and the decisive influence of the internet. By this I don't mean that the internet has not brought many positive developments. But the almost magical possibilities of this technology to communicate worldwide bring with them powerful temptations that threaten the spiritual core of humanity. Good and evil weave into one another in the use of the internet. The Sorat power wants to take possession of human intelligence by constructing a false reality that appears to have more truth to it than living reality. The free intelligence of the human being then becomes the slave of manipulating powers.

The first impetus toward the internet was given in 1969 within the U.S. Department of Defense. Its development accelerated in the 1990s: In 1994 the World Wide Web was introduced, and in 1996 it became a generally accessible phenomenon, without which a global human society has become unthinkable. Those are precisely the years in which Harry Potter's battles with Voldemort are taking place. The culmination of this war with the powers of darkness coincides with the explosive growth of the use of the internet with the symbol *www*. The letter *w* is the Hebrew letter *Vau* and carries the number 6. In this perspective "www" is an indication of "666."

In 1924 Rudolf Steiner described for a limited audience how Sorat continues his work in the rhythm of 666 years:

> During the first 666, dear friends, Sorat was still hidden away inside the evolutionary process of events; he was not seen in any external form, for he lived within the deeds of Arabism, and the initiates were able to see him. When the second 666 years had passed, he showed himself in the thinking and feeling of the tortured Templars. And before this [20th] century is out, he will show himself by making his appearance in many humans as the being by whom they are possessed. [...]

> That is why it is so important that all who are capable of doing so should strive for spirituality. What is inimical to spirituality will be there anyway, for it works not through freedom but under determinism. This determinism has already decreed that at the end of this century Sorat will be on the loose again, so that the intention to sweep away anything spiritual will be deep-seated in large numbers of earthly souls [...]

> ... [L]owered consciousness ... is always a way in for ahrimanic demonic powers, and one of the greatest of these demons is Sorat. Such are the attempts Sorat is making to gain at least temporary access to

the consciousness of human beings in order to bring about calamity and confusion.[22]

From this perspective Harry Potter's battle against evil must not be underestimated. It is a war that started long ago and is continuing all the time. It is clear that without the help of his friends, and especially Dumbledore, Harry would have been lost. In the light of the idea that in Harry Potter the impulse of Mani is working again, who is Dumbledore?

8
Zarathustra and Dumbledore

In chapter 4 we related how Mani lost his life due to the influence of the scholars at the court of Gondishapur who adhered to the rigidified teachings of Zarathustra. Mani, on the other hand, connected the spiritual inheritance of Zarathustra with that of Buddha and advocated a broad view in which the being of Christ as Sun Spirit was paramount. He experienced Zarathustra as his predecessor and fellow warrior.

Zarathustra was said to have had twelve incarnations before he had the name Zoroaster (Golden Star) in his life between 590 and 530 BC in Iran. This series of twelve lives is described in the Nag Hammadi writings that were found in Egypt in 1945. The book about the twelve lives of Zarathustra has the title *The Apocalypse of Adam* and ends with the prediction of the thirteenth life at the beginning of our era.[23]

Zarathustra/Zoroaster, also called Zaradosht, is the builder of the famous fire temple Takht-i-Suleiman in northern Iran. There he taught his disciples that the spirit of the sun, Ahura Mazdao, is engaged in a cosmic battle with Ahriman, the spirit of darkness, for the future of humanity and the earth. Zarathustra's pupils in this temple school were called mages. They wanted to fight for the good through good thoughts, good words and good deeds. Ahriman is the great opponent of the mages in the order of Zarathustra.

The message from *The Apocalypse of Adam* about the incarnation of Zarathustra in the beginning of our era pops up in an expanded version in the 13th century *Book of the Bee* by the Nestorian Christian bishop Solomon of Basra. This book tells how Zarathustra taught a few intimate pupils about a great king who was to be born of a virgin:

> He shall descend from my family; I am he, and he
> is I; he is in me, and I am in him. ... [F]or you will
> be the first to perceive the coming of that great
> king, whom the prisoners await to be set free. Now,
> my sons, guard this secret which I have revealed
> to you, and let it be kept in the treasure-houses of
> your souls. And when that star rises of which I have
> spoken, let ambassadors bearing offerings be sent by
> you [...] He and I are one.[24]

There is a remarkable correspondence between this passage from *The Book of the Bee* and the numerous, very specific statements made by Rudolf Steiner that the Jesus child described in the Gospel of St. Matthew is an incarnation of Zarathustra. As Jesus he created the right conditions for the birth of the Sun Spirit Ahura Mazdao into a human being at the baptism in the Jordan, about thirty years later. It is the spirit of the Sun itself, Christ, who enters into the human being Jesus of Nazareth at the baptism in the Jordan.

In chapter 2 of the Gospel of St. Matthew, we read that wise men from the east (in the Greek text literally called *magi*) guided by a star, find the Jesus child, worship him and honor him with gifts of gold, incense and myrrh. It is quite possible that this "star" was in reality a particular event in the sky, a threefold conjunction of the planets Saturn and Jupiter in the constellation of Pisces, while the sun was in Virgo. According to Babylonian astrologers the Saturn-Jupiter conjunctions order world history.[25]

It is striking that such a threefold conjunction also took place in 1981, the year Harry Potter was born, but now in Virgo with the sun in Pisces, exactly the reverse therefore of the star of the wise men. And just as power-hungry King Herod threatened the life of the newly incarnated Zarathustra, Voldemort tried to kill the infant Harry.

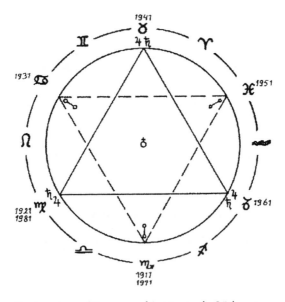

Conjunctions of Saturn and Jupiter in the 20th century: 1921, 1941, 1961, 1981. The last one was a threefold conjunction.

Now that we have seen that Mani possibly lives again in Harry Potter, we can also start looking in Joanne Rowling's epic for the signature of Mani's spiritual teachers, including the individuality of Zarathustra. Then we find the following.

As the son of James and Lily Potter, Harry is born into a circle of magicians. Dumbledore (his full name is Albus Percival Wulfric Brian Dumbledore) has been the headmaster of Hogwarts since 1956 and is also the leader of this circle. In 1970 he founds an order, the Order of the Phoenix. James and Lily Potter, Harry's godfather Sirius Black and many others are members of this order and fight in the sign of the Phoenix when the dark power of Voldemort is growing. Harry will himself also get to know the order.

Raphael Santi, "Zarathustra," detail from The School of Athens, *fresco, Stanza della Segnatura, Vatican, Rome.*

In the Order of Zarathustra, the prophecy was living that one day Ahriman, also called Satan, would incarnate in a human being in order to get humanity in his power through his black-magical intelligence. That incarnation of Ahriman is the theme of the seven Harry Potter books. In Voldemort we can recognize an embodiment of the power of Ahriman. And just as Ahriman was the great opponent of the mages in the Order of Zarathustra, Voldemort is the opponent against which the Order of the Phoenix defends itself. Zarathustra was the most famous white magician of his time.[26] In Albus Dumbledore the spiritual force of Zarathustra is living again, just as Mani seems to manifest himself in Harry. The task begun by the Order of Zarathustra is continued in our time by the Order of the Phoenix.

Dumbledore is exactly 100 years old when Voldemort threatens little Harry's life. From that moment he watches over Harry. Dumbledore is one of the few magicians who have managed to tame a phoenix. Already on his first visit to Dumbledore's room, Harry is deeply impressed by this wonder bird, which burns to ashes time and again but always rises to a new life, thus vanquishing death. During this meeting with the phoenix, Harry seems to come to an inner awareness of the connection with his great teacher that began already before his birth. Just as Mani carried the teaching of Zarathustra in himself from prior lives, in a similar way Harry has from his birth a deep and intense bond with the mission of Dumbledore. We can recognize the relationship of trust that existed between Zarathustra and Mani in the collaboration between Harry and Dumbledore.

In the sixth book, *Harry Potter and the Half-Blood Prince*, set in 1997, Dumbledore is unexpectedly killed. But Harry remains connected with him and experiences the protection emanating from Dumbledore. This is movingly elaborated in the last book, when Harry has a near-death experience and a long conversation with his dead teacher. Harry's decision to return to the earth then leads to the last, decisive fight with Voldemort.

9
Four Leaders of Humanity

In Chapter 5, we related that, as a foster son of a widow, Mani inherited four books from Skythianos that had come into the widow's possession through Terebinthus, a follower of Skythianos. We viewed this story as a picture of spiritual continuity: Skythianos and Terebinthus were predecessors, one could say, brothers of Mani, just like Zarathustra. And it is quite conceivable that Terebinthus was a human being in whom inspiration was working from Gautama Buddha, who was no longer incarnating on earth.

Mani's death in Gondishapur in 276 AD does not in any way mean the end of his mission for humanity. He continued to work, not just by himself, but together with Skythianos, Buddha and Zarathustra. They prepared a new school that would be founded after the year 1000, a school to work in the world with white magic developed through Christ who connected Himself with the earth. Rudolf Steiner sketches this collaboration:

> It is said that a few centuries after Christ lived
> on the earth, there was held one of the greatest
> assemblies of the spiritual world connected with the
> earth that ever took place, and that there Manes[27]
> gathered round him three mighty personalities of
> the fourth century after Christ. [...] Who were these

personalities brought together by Manes in that memorable assembly? (It should be remembered that such an event can be witnessed only by spiritual sight.) He called together the personality in whom Skythianos lived at that time, and also the physical reflection of the Buddha who had then appeared again, and the erstwhile Zarathustra who was wearing a physical body at that time. Around Manes was this council, himself in the center and around him Skythianos, Buddha and Zarathustra. And in that council a plan was agreed upon for causing all the wisdom of the Bodhisattvas of the post-Atlantean time to flow more and more strongly into the future of mankind; and the plan of the future evolution of the civilizations of the earth then decided upon was adhered to and carried over into the European mysteries of the Rose Cross. These particular mysteries have always been connected with the individualities of Skythianos, Buddha and Zarathustra. They were the teachers in the schools of the Rose Cross.[28]

Rudolf Steiner lifts a tip of the veil that hides the mysterious individuality of Skythianos when he describes him as a being that cannot easily be identified as a human being:

This clairvoyance could not develop further; it withdrew perforce into separate personalities in the West. It was guided by a Being who once upon a time lived in deepest concealment, withdrawn behind those who had already forsaken the world and who were pupils of the great initiates. This Being had remained behind in order to preserve for later ages what was brought over from old Atlantis. Among the great initiates who had founded mystery places in the West for the preservation of the old Atlantean wisdom, a wisdom that entered deeply into all the secrets of the physical body, was the great Skythianos, as he was called in the Middle Ages.[29]

Ever since the events around the birth of the Jesus child at the beginning of our era, Zarathustra has been connected with Buddha. Since then, Buddha and Zarathustra have had the great task of bringing together the followers of the two different magical-spiritual streams of which they are the leaders. These two streams are expressed in the shepherds described in the Gospel of St. Luke and the wise men of the Gospel of St. Matthew. Buddha irradiated the hearts of the shepherds with his compassion and love; with his wisdom and goodness, Zarathustra led the wise men through his star. As we saw in the previous chapter, Zarathustra is represented in the Harry Potter books in the person of Dumbledore, the wise and good protector of the pupils at Hogwarts. And Skythianos and Buddha—are they also represented?

In the way Rudolf Steiner sketches Skythianos, there is much to remind us of Rubeus Hagrid, modest as he is. Hagrid is also not a normal human being; he is a half-giant of enormous size and superhuman strength. Beings the size of Hagrid are described in legends of old Atlantis. Hagrid is very popular among the readers of the Harry Potter books. He has a golden heart and knows the ancient secrets of nature, of herbs and metals, and of dragons and centaurs. Beings like that disappeared from the face of the earth with the demise of Atlantis, but in the forests around Hogwarts they are living on. Indeed, Hagrid is the guardian of ancient Atlantean wisdom. From a spiritual point of view, this brings him in the immediate vicinity of Skythianos.

51

Terebinthus could be the secret name of Sirius Black, Harry's godfather and sworn friend of Harry's father, James, and Remus Lupin. Sirius is the name of a bright star, also called the Dog Star, in the constellation of Canis Minor, Little Dog. And indeed, Sirius Black is able to change his shape into that of a black dog. He has mastered this capacity, which is really a sacrifice, out of solidarity with his friend Remus Lupin, who was bitten by a werewolf and has to change into a werewolf at every full moon. As a dog Sirius can accompany Remus so that, as a werewolf, he cannot do any harm. Sirius makes sacrifices as only Gautama Buddha was able to do. There is a legend about Buddha that one day he gave his life for some hungry Brahmans by changing into a hare.

There is also another indication that puts Sirius in the spiritual vicinity of Buddha. Before Buddha accomplished his final task in India, he worked in the north of Europe as the god Wotan:

> The same being who was called Wotan in Germanic myths appeared again as Buddha. Buddha and Wotan are even related linguistically.[30]

In the Norse and Germanic myths, Wotan is accompanied and faithfully served on his travels by two black wolfhounds. In precisely the shape of a black wolfhound, Sirius saves Harry's life in the third book, *Harry Potter and the Prisoner of Azkaban*. Full of compassion and loving readiness to sacrifice, in the spirit of Buddha, Sirius always risks everything to assist Harry. He could be a physical reflection of Buddha, just like the second, nameless, participant in the spiritual conference of four leaders of humanity called by Mani around 300 AD.

Just as Mani collaborates with Zarathustra, Skythianos and Buddha since their great spiritual conference, Harry finds at Hogwarts, as in a supersensible mystery school, friends and teachers in Albus Dumbledore, Rubeus Hagrid and Sirius Black, who have placed unconditional faithfulness and hope in him. In the battles with Voldemort, who tries to turn Hogwarts into a School of Black Magic in the spirit of Gondishapur, they stand around Harry. Voldemort would like it most of all if, for all the pupils of Hogwarts, the renunciation formula would be introduced that the Church used in the Middle Ages against suspected followers of Mani: "I abjure Zarathustra, Buddha and Skythianos." These three individualities work together with the reborn Mani out of the white sun forces of wisdom, love and goodness.

10

Harry Potter and Parzival

In August 1980, a few weeks after Harry Potter was born on July 31, I heard a new perception of Mani from professor Bernard Lievegoed, who was then 75 years old. The lecture he gave then is unforgettable for me because, in speaking about Mani, he made a statement that has remained a lasting life reality for me ever since. He said that Mani was born again in the ninth century as the historical Parzival. As Parzival he was connected with the secret of the Grail. And also in our time, he is the initiate who accompanies the seekers of the Grail on their path. Rudolf Steiner said the following about the relation between Mani and Parzival:

> During his life as Manes, this soul worked to
> prepare for his real future mission: to bring about
> the true reconciliation of all religions. To achieve
> this he had to be born again as a soul with a very
> special relationship to the Christ. All that had arisen
> in his soul as ancient and new knowledge during his
> lifetime as Manes had to become submerged again.
> As the "innocent fool," the soul inevitably had to
> confront the external knowledge of the world and
> the working of Christ in the depths of its being. He
> was born again as Parzival, the son of Herzeleide ...[31]

Between 1200 and 1208, Wolfram von Eschenbach told his version of the Parzival epic in many castles in Central

Parzival

Europe. His words indicate that the historical Parzival lived in the ninth century, the time when the Carolingian Empire was formed. We may conclude this from what he says about Parzival's mother, namely, that she lived eleven generations before his own time: "Alas that we do not now possess her descendants down to the eleventh branch!"[32]

Wolfram figured 33 years for a generation, after the life of Jesus Christ on earth. Thus starting from 1200 we go back 11 x 33 years = 363 years, to arrive at the generation of the mother of Parzival, Herzeleide. Parzival himself then follows 33 years later, approximately between 837 and 870. Thus Parzival was alive at the time of the Council of Constantinople, where the weighty prohibition against speaking of the independent spirit of the human being was proclaimed. Wolfram could tell the Parzival story with such exactitude only because he was himself an initiate: "When you open Wolfram von Eschenbach's books you will see everywhere that he was an initiate."[33]

Mani continued his task in his next life. He had to be born in deep secrecy so that the Prince of Darkness would not find him right away. Even his name must not become known. His mother Herzeleide had a dream before his birth that he was being threatened by a murderous dragon. She wanted to protect him from all evil and did not tell him his true name. Wolfram tells about Parzival that he grew up as the "son of a widow"—that was also how Mani was known. Parzival's father, Gamuret, was killed in a battle near Baghdad.

Thus the child grew up without knowing his descent as heir to a kingdom and of a long expected future kingship of the Grail. His mother called him "dear boy." But toward his twelfth year she could no longer hold him back. Parzival heard of King Arthur and wanted to go to him, to learn and become an Arthurian Knight. The departure of her son broke Herzeleide's heart, and she died without Parzival's realizing it as he rode away. But because of this she could accompany him spiritually on all his travels and in all his battles, so that her beloved child ultimately did reach his goal and destiny.

This same motif is also the secret of Harry Potter. His mother Lily gives her life in order to save little Harry from Voldemort. Exactly this substitute dying enables her to protect Harry again and again against Voldemort and his black magic. Just like Parzival, Harry grows up in a hidden place, with the Dursley family. And just like Parzival he begins the training that leads him to his destiny only after his eleventh birthday, in the twelfth year of his life.

The great task the Arthurian Knights attempted to accomplish was the battle against demons in the dark and wild forests of Western Europe. They wanted to bring light into the darkness. Parzival travels this path, a path that leads through doubt to inner peace, *saelde*. It is a path that can be traveled only through mildness, and on which the personality becomes transparent to the Sun Spirit which, as a pure force, works in the Grail. *Saelde* is reached when the soul is permeated by the fire of the Spirit. The subtle etheric effect of the Grail is the good that vanquishes evil through love. It is the working of the Christ.

When Mani-Parzival enters the secret Grail Castle, he meets its old builder and the original leader of the Order of the Grail. His name is Titurel. This is the reborn Zarathustra: "Titurel is the one who left at the time Christ descended to earth: the Zarathustra individuality."[34] The expression "left at the time Christ descended to earth" refers to the fact that the individuality of Zarathustra withdrew from the soul of Jesus of Nazareth before the baptism in the Jordan, in order to cede its place to the Christ as the Spirit of the Sun. As Jesus, the reborn Zarathustra prepared for thirty years the soul that was to serve as a vessel for the Spirit of the Sun. Similarly, every human being can now develop the soul in such a way that he can say, like the man Jesus: "Not I, but the higher I, the Sun Spirit in me." This is precisely the secret that was guarded in the Order of the Grail.

Wolfram von Eschenbach writes about this order:

> The host said: "It is well known to me that
> many a valorous hand resides by the Grail at
> Montsalvaesche. In search of adventure they
> constantly ride many a journey. Those same
> templars, wherever they meet with grief or fame,
> they count it against their sins. A combative
> company dwells there. I will tell you of their food:
> They live by a stone whose nature is most pure.

If you know nothing of it, it shall be named to you here: it is called *lapsit exillis*.[35] By that stone's power the phoenix burns away, turning to ashes, yet those ashes bring it back to life. Thus the phoenix sheds its molting plumage and thereafter gives off so much bright radiance that it becomes as beautiful as before. Moreover, never was a man in such pain but from that day he beholds the stone, he cannot die in the week that follows immediately after. [...] Such power does the stone bestow upon a man that his flesh and bone immediately acquire youth. That stone is also called the Grail.[36]

Here we have the story of the Phoenix: It dies and then rises again from its own ashes by the power of the Grail. In this way the individual spirit of the human being is immortal and embodies itself again and again in a soul and a body. As a result of the Council of Constantinople, this insight disappeared from general awareness. But in the Order of the Grail it was preserved. In his time, Parzival fought for the recognition of the spirit.

In *Harry Potter and the Order of the Phoenix,* we read how Harry falls in with the order Albus Dumbledore had founded to oppose Voldemort in the sign of the Phoenix. This was the book that confirmed for me the connection of Dumbledore and Harry with the secret of the Grail. Just like the Order of the Grail, one could not find the Order of the Phoenix on one's own power; one had to be led to it. In truth, the Order of the Phoenix is really a picture for the continued working of the Order of the Grail in our time. And now again, in our time, it is Mani-Parzival who is the guardian of this ideal of the Grail.

Parzival met Titurel, the old leader of the Order of the Grail, when he entered the Grail Castle for the first time, just as Harry met Dumbledore when he entered Hogwarts. Did the old, old Titurel know that Parzival would ultimately become the new leader of the Order of the Grail? Did he realize that Parzival would have to experience years of battle and trial first? Titurel was to die at the moment when Parzival was mature enough for his task as leader and guardian of the Order of the Grail. Did Albus Dumbledore also realize that Harry would continue his task when this inconspicuous young boy entered Hogwarts for the first time in the beginning of his twelfth year? Did he know that one day Harry Potter would take over his task? Has that moment come, now [2011] that Harry Potter is 31 years old?

11

Harry Potter in 2011

In 1924 Ehrenfried Pfeiffer (1899–1961) asked Rudolf Steiner whether Mani was on earth at that time. According to Rudolf Steiner that was not the case. But he added:

> Mani will not incarnate during this [20th] century, but he intends to do so in the next century—if he can find a suitable body. The ordinary kind of education does not provide any possibility for Mani to develop; only Waldorf education will do so. If the right conditions are provided, he will appear as a teacher of humankind and take up leadership in matters of art and religion. He will act from the power of the Grail mysteries, and he will instruct humankind so that they may decide even about good and evil.[37]

Bernard Lievegoed, a friend of Ehrenfried Pfeiffer's, elaborated on this statement:

> By karma, Manes' incarnation would be due by the end of the [20th] century. [...] Such an incarnation would bring about a complete change of trend in history. People fool around with things like the United Nations, and don't know how to solve world problems. We have to overcome the trial-and-error method in political activity and change it based on reason, understanding and wisdom.[38]

Harry Potter was born in 1980, in the last part of the 20th century. Harry bestowed a mighty intuition on Joanne Rowling during her train journey to London in 1990. With great commitment and persistence, Joanne Rowling transformed her encounter with the boyish face in the rain-spattered train window into a spiritual work of art through which young and old all over the world feel connected. She said:

> ... I knew that unless I made a push to finish the
> first book now, I might never finish it. I made a
> huge, superhuman effort. I would put Jessica in
> her pushchair, take her to the park and try to tire
> her out. When she fell asleep I'd rush to a café and
> write. Not all the cafés I went to approved of my
> sitting there for a couple of hours having bought
> only one cup of coffee [...] The first agent I sent the
> manuscript to returned it. The first publisher I sent
> the manuscript to returned it. So I sent it off again.
> The second agent, Christopher Little, took it on—his
> letter is one of the best I have ever received. It took
> a year to find a publisher but when Bloomsbury
> accepted it, it was definitely the second best
> moment in my life—after Jessica. A year later, July
> 1997, the book was finally published.[39]

Since the last Harry Potter film came out in July 2011, the attention Harry received in the outer world will probably quiet down. He was then in his 31st year. Who is Harry Potter?

That is the question I have tried to answer in this little book. I found Harry's true identity in Mani and in the continuation of his mission as Parzival. This answer is only a preliminary one. What I am hoping for is that, after reading this booklet, the readers will begin their own investigations.

One thing is a certainty for me: The real Harry Potter is alive and working as our contemporary for a better world in which love can work effectively. The Harry Potter story shows in pictures real events that have been happening in the world since 1980. We have to do with a spiritual battle being fought behind the scenes of outer reality, a battle in service of humanity and the good future of the earth. Great initiates such as Mani and Zarathustra are involved in this battle. The reality of this battle is apparently understood by a great many readers at an instinctive level.

The real Harry Potter inspired Joanne Rowling with these pictures on that rainy journey in 1990. Let us hope that he can continue his task in the service of free intelligence and of an existence worthy of human beings in a time when the power of dark manipulation is frightfully great. The Harry Potter story shows that, in the end, the power of mildness and love is victorious. We can try what we want with the intellect, understanding and wisdom, but ultimately the most magical force for the good is love. Harry Potter learns in the battle with Voldemort that love is the power of the white magician.

> "Is it love again?" said Voldemort, his snake's face
> jeering. "Dumbledore's favorite solution, *love*,
> which he claimed conquered death, though love did
> not stop him falling from the tower and breaking
> like an old waxwork? *Love*, which did not prevent
> me stamping out your Mudblood mother like a
> cockroach, Potter—and nobody seems to love you
> enough to run forward this time and take my curse.
> So what will stop you dying now when I strike?"[40]

During her interview with Oprah Winfrey in the fall of 2010,[41] Joanne Rowling was very clear: "What counts for me is the love that is victorious." And in a few sentences she connected this with genuine Christianity. She admitted that her conviction "that love is victorious" is the central theme of the Harry Potter books, and that this is true for the real content of all religions, without exception. She added immediately that she had no intention of converting anyone and had, for that reason, written the books without referring to any religion at all.

In the last chapter of the seventh book, we see Harry and his beloved Ginny with their three children standing on platform 9¾ of King's Cross Station. They are taking Albus, their eldest son, to the Hogwarts Express. Hogwarts is in full swing again, and the train departs on September 1. It is time to go; the connection between the two worlds has been accomplished without evil getting the upper hand. A golden future is shining ahead: Religion and art have been transformed into spiritual revelation and creative spiritual power that will bring a better future for the world. "The scar had not pained Harry for nineteen years. All was well."

Endnotes

1. http://video.the-leaky-cauldron.org/video/1629.

2. In the United States this book was published with the title *Harry Potter and the Sorcerer's Stone.*

3. Lindsey Fraser, *Conversations with J.K. Rowling*, Scholastic Press, 2000.

4. http://members.chello.nl/~h.kip/werkstuk/page21.html, transl. PM.

5. Rudolf Steiner, *Karmic Relationships*, Vol. III, GA 237, lecture of August 1, 1924.

6   Ibid.

7. Rudolf Steiner, *Death as Metamorphosis of Life*, GA 182, lecture 7, "How Can I Find the Christ?" Zurich, October 16, 1918.

8. Rudolf Steiner, *The Book of Revelation and the Work of the Priest*, GA 346, lecture of September 20, 1924.

9. Rudolf Steiner, *The Temple Legend*, GA 93, lecture 6, "Manichaeism," November 11, 1904.

10. Hans Jonas, *Het Gnosticisme [Gnosticism]*, Spectrum: Utrecht, Netherlands, 1969.

11. Gilles Quispel (1916–2006) was a Dutch theologian and historian of Christianity and Gnosticism. He became

professor of early Christian history at Utrecht University. He worked on the Gospel of Thomas and was closely associated with the editing of the Nag Hammadi Library.

12. From an article by the author in the periodical *Vrije Opvoedkunst* [Waldorf Education], 2005, no. 5.

13. J. Oort & G. Quispel, *The Cologne Mani Codex*, Amsterdam, 2005.

14. Op. cit., Jonas.

15. Ibid.

16. www.fas.harvard.edu/~iranian/Manicheism/ Manicheism_II_Texts.pdf (Shabuhragan; BT 11 no. 5.1 M 49 MM ii, pages 307–082 [How to live a good life]).

17. Op. cit., Steiner, *The Temple Legend*, note 8: quoted from notes of another, unspecified lecture.

18. Rudolf Steiner, *Die Polarität von Dauer und Entwickelung im Menschenleben [The Polarity of Duration and Development in Human Life]*, GA 184, Dornach, 1968.

19. Op. cit., Steiner, *The Temple Legend*.

20. Rudolf Steiner, *Inner Impulses of Evolution*, GA 171, Lecture of September 25, 1916.

21. Agrippa von Nettesheim, *Die magischen Werke [The Works of Magic]*, Wiesbaden, 1988.

22. Op. cit., Steiner, *The Book of Revelation and the Work of the Priest*, lecture of September 12, 1924.

23. Andrew Welburn, *The Book with Fourteen Seals. The Prophet Zarathustra and the Christ Revelation*, Rudolf Steiner Press, 1991.

24. www.sacred-texts.com/chr/bb: *Book of the Bee*, translated by E.A. Wallis Budge, 1886, chapter 37.

25. Walter Bühler, *Der Stern der Weisen [The Star of the Wise Men]*, Stuttgart, 1983.

26. D. van Bemmelen, *Zarathoestra, de eerste profeet van Christus [Zarathustra, the First Prophet of Christ]*, Zeist, 1967.

27. In different traditions Mani is also called Manes.

28. Rudolf Steiner, *The East in the Light of the West*, GA 113, Chapter IX.

29. Ibid.

30. Rudolf Steiner, *Egyptian Myths and Mysteries*, GA 106, lecture 10.

31. Rudolf Steiner, *From the History and Contents of the First Section of the Esoteric School 1904–1914*, GA 264, Anthroposophic Press, 1998, page 218.

32. Wolfram von Eschenbach, *Parzival*, Book III-128, tr. Cyril Edwards, Oxford World Classics.

33. Rudolf Steiner, *Die okkulten Wahrheiten alter Mythen und Sagen [The Occult Truths of Ancient Myths and Sagas]*, GA 92, Dornach, 1999.

34. From Elisabeth Vreede's notes of Rudolf Steiner's esoteric lesson of August 27, 1909; not reported in *Esoteric Lessons 1904–1909*, GA 266/1.

35. A corrupt Latin term; its sense would seem to be "It fell from the heavens."

36. Op. cit., von Eschenbach, *Parzival*, Book IX-469.

37. Op. cit., Steiner, *From the History and Contents*, page 227.

38. Ehrenfried Pfeiffer, *Notes and Lectures Compendium I*, Mercury Press, 1991.

39. Op. cit., Fraser.

40. J.K. Rowling, *Harry Potter and the Deathly Hallows*, page 739.

41. Op. cit., http://video.the-leaky-cauldron.org.

Bibliography

BOOKS

D. van Bemmelen, *Zarathoestra, de eerste profeet van Christus*, Zeist, 1967.

E. Bock, *Childhood of Jesus*, Edinburgh, 1997.

W. Bühler, *Der Stern der Weisen*, Stuttgart, 1983.

Zeylmans van Emmichoven, *De werkelijkheid waarin wij leven*, Amsterdam, 1993.

W. von Eschenbach, *Parzival*, translated by Cyril Edwards, Oxford, 2009.

L. Fraser, *Conversations with J.K. Rowling*, Scholastic Press, 2000.

J. Huizinga, *Collected Works, Vol. 4*, Haarlem, 1953.

J. W. von Goethe, *Faust – A Tragedy*, translated by Bayard Taylor, New York, 1950.

H. Jonas, *Het Gnosticisme [Gnosticism]*, Utrecht, 1969.

A. von Keyserlingk, *Die Reise nach Byzanz; Das Palladium des Sieges*, Basel, 1991.

D. Koelman, *Graal en Foenix*, Rotterdam, 1993.

B. Lievegoed, *The Battle for the Soul*, Stroud, 1994.

F. Lutters, *Daniel van Bemmelen 1899–1982, Opnieuw geboren aan het begin van het Lichte Tijdperk*, Driebergen, 2005.

_____ , *Een werkelijke ontmoeting*, Vrije Opvoedkunst, Driebergen, 2005.

A. von Nettesheim, *Die magischen Werke*, Wiesbaden, 1988.

J. Oort & G. Quispel, *De Keulse Mani Codex*, Amsterdam, 2006.

E. Pfeiffer, *Notes and Lectures*, Spring Valley, 1991.

M. Ploeger, *Francisco d'Almeida en de weg naar het onbekende*, Zeist, 1992.

L. Ravagli, *Die Geheime Botschaft der Joanne K. Rowling*, Stuttgart, 2007.

L. Ringbom, *Graltempel und Paradies*, Stockholm, 1951.

J.K. Rowling, *Harry Potter and the Chamber of Secrets*, Scholastic Press, 1999.

_____ , *Harry Potter and the Deathly Hallows*, Scholastic Press, 2007.

_____ , *Harry Potter and the Goblet of Fire*, Scholastic Press, 2000.

_____ , *Harry Potter and the Half-Blood Prince*, Scholastic Press, 2005.

_____ , *Harry Potter and the Order of the Phoenix*, Scholastic Press, 2003.

_____ , *Harry Potter and the Philosopher's Stone*, Scholastic Press, 1997.

_____ , *Harry Potter and the Prisoner of Azkaban*, Scholastic Press, 1999.

H. Schoffler, *Die Akademie von Gondishapur*, Stuttgart, 1979.

J. Slavenburg & W. Glaudemans, *De Nag Hammadi Geschriften*, Deventer, 2005.

A. Steffen, *Das Todeserlebnis des Manes*, Dornach, 1934.

W. Stein, *Graalschrift no. 5*, Leiden, 1988.

W.J. Stein, *The Ninth Century*, London, 1991.

Rudolf Steiner, *The Book of Revelation and the Work of the Priest*, GA 346, London, 1998.

_____ , *Death as Metamorphosis of Life*, GA 182, Great Barrington, 2008.

_____ , *The East in the Light of the West*, GA 113, London, 1940.

_____ , *Egyptian Myths and Mysteries*, GA 106, New York, 1971.

_____ , *Esoteric Christianity*, GA 130, London, 1984.

_____ , *From the History and Contents of the First Esoteric School 1904–1914*, GA 264, Great Barrington, 1998.

_____ , *Inner Impulses of Evolution*, GA 171, Hudson, 1984.

_____ , *Karmic Relationships, Vol. III*, GA 237, London, 1957.

_____ , *Die okkulten Wahrheiten alter Mythen und Sagen*, GA 92, Dornach, 1999.

_____ , *Die Polarität von Dauer und Entwickelung*, GA 184, Dornach, 1968.

_____ , *The Reappearance of Christ in the Etheric*, GA 118, Great Barrington, 2003.

_____ , *The Temple Legend*, GA 93, London, 1985.

C. Tacitus, *Sämtliche Werke*, Annalen XIV, Vienna, 1935.

R. van Vliet, *Manicheisme als het Christendom van vrijheid en liefde*, Kampen, 2000.

A. Welburn, *The Book with Fourteen Seals. The Prophet Zarathustra and the Christ Revelation*, Sussex, 1991.

WEBSITES

http://www.fas.harvard.edu/~iranian.Manicheism/ Manicheism_II_Texts. pdfShabuhragan; BT 11 no. 5.1 MM ii, pp. 307–082.

http://en.wikipedia.org/wiki/List_of_best-selling_books.

http://harvardmagazine.com/2008/06/the-fringe-benefits-failure-the-importance-imagination.

http://nl.wikipedia.org/wiki/Harry_Potter.

http://members.chello.nl/~h.kip/werkstuk/page21/html.

http://triangulum.nl/Bijdragen/Verschijnselen/Siemes%20 bethlehem.html.

http://video.the-leaky-cauldron.org/video/1629.

http://www.humanities.uci.edu/sasanika/pdf/Kephalaia.pdf.

http://www.xs4all.nl/~carlkop/wonder.html.

http://www.sacred-texts.com/chr/bb: *Book of the Bee*, translated by E.A. Wallis Budge, 1886.